Imperium Latin
Puzzles

Julian Morgan

Edition 1.0.1

All photographs used in this book were taken
by the Author, with the sanction
of the institutions involved.

Any errors and omissions in this book are
the fault of the Author. They will be rectified
as soon as he becomes aware of them.

DEDICATION

For Joka with all my love

ACKNOWLEDGEMENTS

My thanks go to all who helped in checking the manuscript of this book. In particular, thanks go to Edward Barber, Joka Morgan, Victoria Steckhan and Kateryna Trybushna

CONTENTS

PART 1

Puzzles based on Imperium Latin Book 1

1   Meet the folks

See if you can complete the grid below and by so doing, find out the person whose name goes down the middle of the grid.

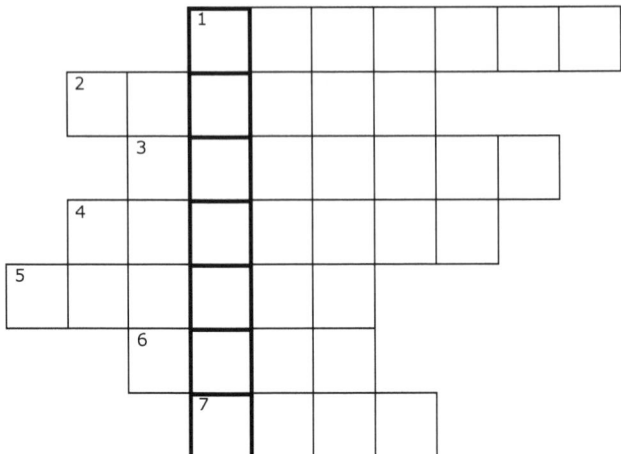

1.   Hadrian's mother (7)
2.   Hadrian's family name (6)
3.   Hadrian's sister's first name (7)
4.   Trajan's niece (7)
5.   Trajan's family name (6)
6.   Trajan's maidservant (4)
7.   Hadrian's father (4)

The name going down the grid is: ....

2   Names wordsearch

Find the names and places from the list below, which have all been hidden in the grid.

E	R	R	D	N	I	T	A	L	I	C	A
F	E	U	O	C	Y	J	L	X	M	N	E
W	F	C	M	A	T	I	D	I	A	V	M
A	A	W	I	D	S	T	S	Q	R	H	O
P	L	O	T	I	N	A	I	D	C	T	R
B	T	G	I	Z	P	L	I	Z	U	N	G
A	T	R	A	A	N	I	B	A	S	Q	E
I	G	A	P	E	D	C	W	F	R	U	N
N	L	E	A	R	I	U	S	E	T	A	S
A	E	C	U	B	L	I	E	D	I	E	T
P	R	U	L	P	U	N	T	R	R	L	I
S	A	L	I	Q	A	E	D	O	N	I	A
I	R	U	N	A	J	A	R	T	H	U	R
H	S	S	A	T	H	V	W	E	W	S	T

Aelius	Hadrian	Plotina
Afer	Hispania	Rome
Cadiz	Italica	Sabina
Domitia Paulina	Marcus	Trajan
Graeculus	Matidia	Ulpius

3   English to Latin crossword

The clues are in English but your answers should be in Latin.

Across

1. Two (3)
2. You (pl) are (5)
5. Houses (acc pl) (5)
6. To control (9)
10. You (s) fear (5)
11. You (pl) give (5)
12. I (3)

Down

1. She leads (5)
2. You (s) wait for (9)
3. Earth (5)
4. I am (3)
7. He moves (5)
8. And I stand (2,3)
9. But (3)

4

4   Sudoku

You know how Sudoku works. All you have to do is to place numbers one to nine in each vertical and horizontal line and then make sure that each number appears once in each of the nine 3x3 squares. The difference here is that this is Roman Sudoku!

You use the numbers as below:

1	2	3	4	5	6	7	8	9
I	II	III	IV	V	VI	VII	VIII	IX

	VI			III		IX		I
IX	III	VIII	I		VII	V		VI
							VIII	II
III			VI		I		V	
				VII		VIII		
	VIII		V		III			VII
VI	I			IV				
VIII		III	II		V	IV	I	IX
V		IV		I			III	

5

5   Sadly I sit

*The object of the puzzle is to find out which letter of the alphabet is represented by each of the 16 numbers used. You are given two words to start you off, so you can begin by entering any letters from these wherever they appear in the grid. Each word you make should be in good Latin. As you decode each letter, write it in the **Letters deciphered** table and cross it off in the **Letters used** table.*

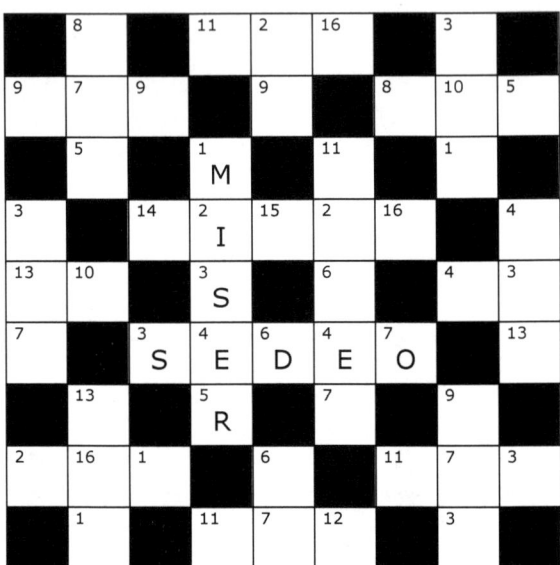

Letters deciphered

1	2	3	4	5	6	7	8	9	10	11	12	13	14	15	16
M	I	S	E	R	D	O									

Letters used

A	C	D	E	F	I	L	M	N	O	R	S	T	U	V	X

6   English to Latin crossword

The clues are in English but your answers should be in Latin.

Across

4. Quickly (9)
6. Angry (f) (5)
7. And I (2,3)
9. Now (3)
10. It gives (3)
11. We (3)
14. Cities (5)
15. They do (5)
17. Worried (f) (9)

Down

1. Weep! (pl) (5)
2. To go (3)
3. Stand! (pl) (5)
4. Why a bull? (3,6)
5. I ask all things (4,5)
8. So (3)
12. Chair (5)
13. From fields (5)
16. Road (3)

7   Latin to English crossword

The clues are in Latin but your answers should be in English.

Across

6. ager (5)
7. agis (3,2)
8. terra (5)
10. sede in (3,2)
13. ad (2)
15. ianua (1,4)
16. i (2)
19. neco (1,4)
22. milita (5)
23. ad mare (2,3)
25. audio (1,4)

Down

1. post (5)
2. cor (5)
3. nobis (2,2)
4. debeo (4)
5. de (4)
9. ad omnes (2,3)
11. urgeo (1,4)
12. sum (1,2)
14. roga (3)
17. iube (5)
18. sumus (2,3)
19. in (+ acc) (4)
20. rogo (1,3)
21. ducite (4)

8   Spanish connections

See if you can complete the grid below and by so doing, find out the person whose name goes down the middle of it.

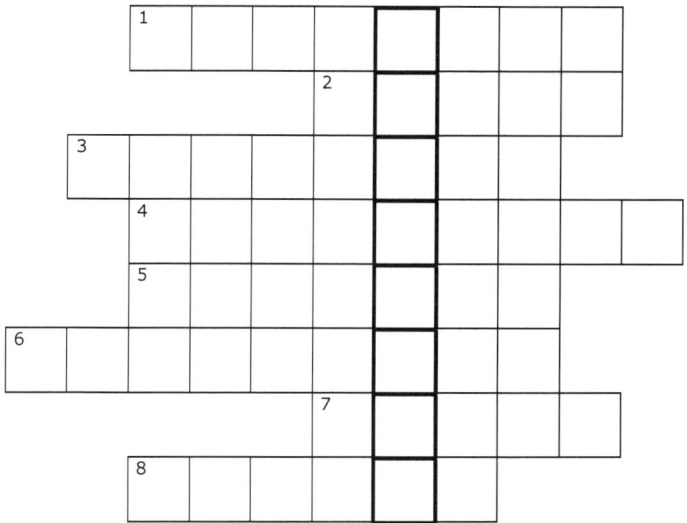

1. Rome's main rival in the third century BC (8)
2. Where Hannibal grew fat (5)
3. An early Roman province (8)
4. Trajan built a bridge there (9)
5. Another early Roman province (7)
6. He founded New Carthage (9)
7. The river where Trajan built 4 Across (5)
8. Rome's first province (6)

The name going down the grid is: ....

9   ArrowWord

All the clues are on the grid. The answers should all be in Latin.

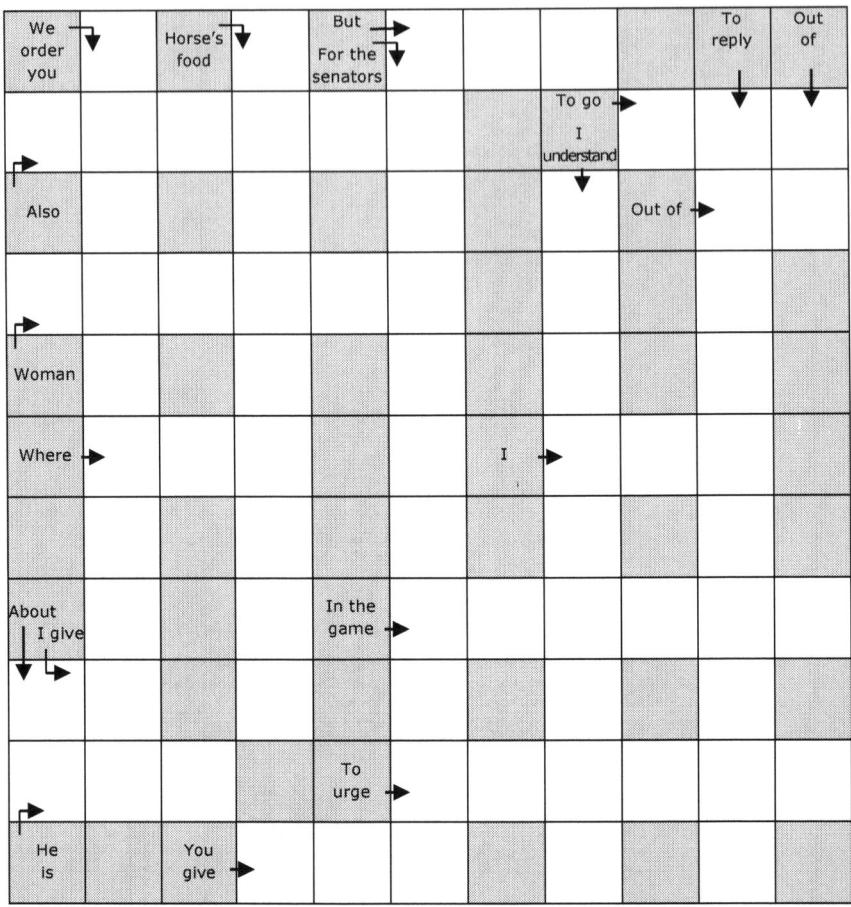

10   English to Latin crossword

The clues are in English but your answers should be in Latin.

Across

4. You are new (2,5,2)
6. All of it (4)
7. For all (4)
8. Dangerous (n) (11)
9. Sea (4)
11. For bread (4)
12. Hold the bear! (4,5)

Down

1. In myself (2,2)
2. Of the uncles (11)
3. Be! (4)
4. They control (9)
5. Blood (acc) (9)
10. They go (4)
11. After (4)

11   Latin to English crossword

The clues are in Latin but your answers should be in English.

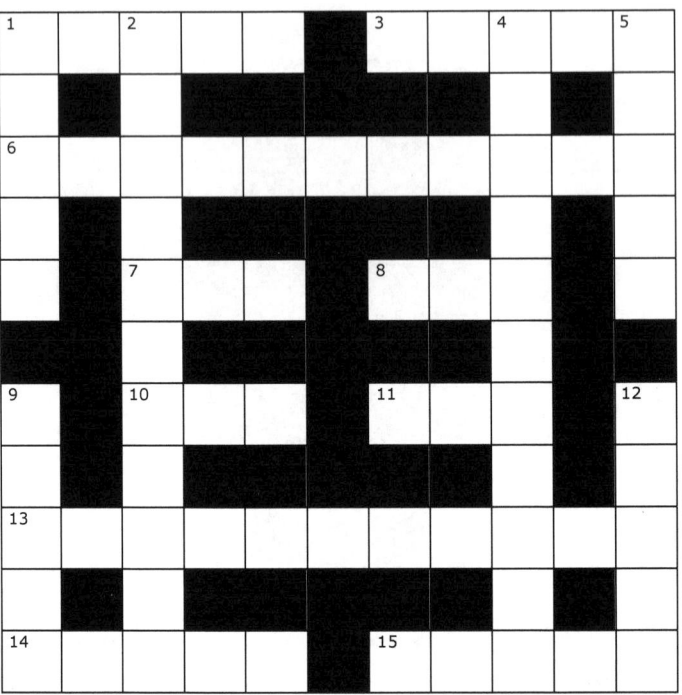

Across

1. ursae (5)
3. tauri (5)
6. iubet ursas (6,5)
7. devora! (3)
8. filius (3)
10. iace (3)
11. eo (1,2)
13. vias amamus (5,2,4)
14. somnium (5)
15. mitto (1,4)

Down

1. sanguis (5)
2. et nos placemus (3,2,6)
4. disce amare (5,2,4)
5. tam miser (2,3)
9. fessus (5)
12. panis (5)

12   We hear the waters

*The object of the puzzle is to find out which letter of the alphabet is represented by each of the 16 numbers used. You are given two words to start you off, so you can begin by entering any letters from these wherever they appear in the grid. Each word you make should be in good Latin. As you decode each letter, write it in the **Letters deciphered** table and cross it off in the **Letters used** table.*

Letters deciphered

1	2	3	4	5	6	7	8	9	10	11	12	13	14	15	16
A	U	D	I	M	S	Q									

Letters used

A	B	C	D	E	I	L	M	N	O	P	Q	R	S	T	U

13 Sudoku

You know how Sudoku works. All you have to do is to place numbers one to nine in each vertical and horizontal line and then make sure that each number appears once in each of the nine 3x3 squares. The difference here is that this is Roman Sudoku!

You use the numbers as below:

1	2	3	4	5	6	7	8	9
I	II	III	IV	V	VI	VII	VIII	IX

		I	III	V			IX	
	IX			I		VI	III	V
			VII	VIII	IV	I		
	III	V			VII			IX
				III				
VI			I			III	IV	
	VII	VIII	V	IV				
IX	II	IV		VIII			VII	
	V			IX	I	II		

14   Politics and History wordsearch

Find the words from the list below, which have all been hidden in the grid.

V	I	A	A	P	P	I	A	N	R	G	H
I	C	H	A	N	N	I	B	A	L	L	D
C	P	A	N	V	U	R	O	A	D	A	R
Z	R	L	C	F	R	V	R	I	B	D	O
E	O	U	T	A	T	E	E	K	R	I	W
N	V	G	V	A	R	E	N	A	N	A	S
U	I	I	W	Y	G	T	J	C	K	T	N
T	N	L	T	R	L	I	H	Z	V	O	E
P	C	A	L	I	G	I	L	A	I	R	D
E	E	C	Q	E	Y	N	C	H	G	R	O
N	X	D	M	V	M	W	O	I	R	E	O
O	A	T	I	H	L	L	O	R	S	Z	W
C	O	L	O	S	S	E	U	M	J	F	F
I	B	V	V	E	S	P	A	S	I	A	N

arena	Hannibal	province
Caligula	Livy	Sicily
Carthage	Neptune	Vespasian
Colosseum	Nero	Via Appia
gladiator	Nerva	wooden sword

15   Not so polite

See if you can complete the grid below and by so doing, find out the syntactical term which goes down the middle of it.

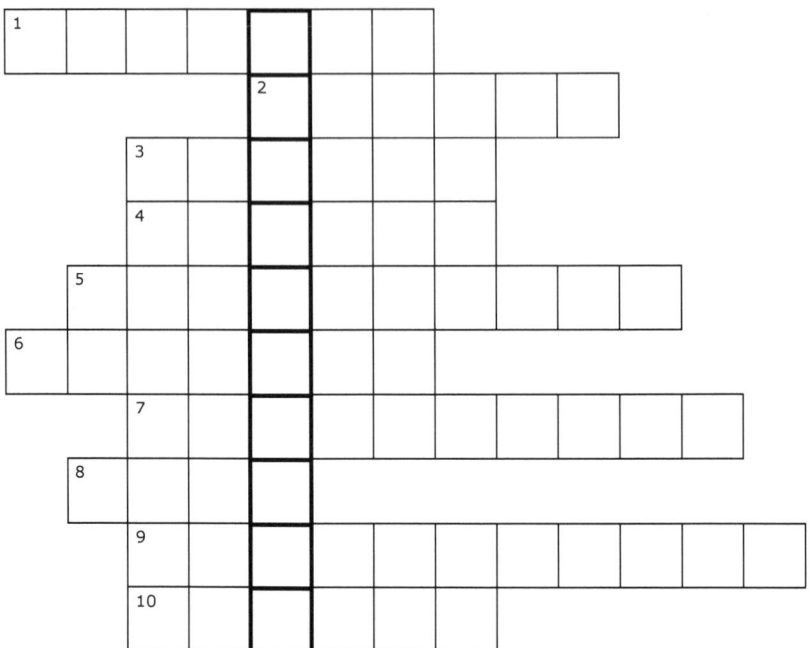

1. A word like *a* or *the* (7)
2. It is usually in the Accusative (6)
3. Both Masculine and Feminine (6)
4. The fourth principal part of a verb (6)
5. A group of nouns (10)
6. It performs the action of a verb (7)
7. Use this in Latin for 6 (10)
8. The Ablative is one (4)
9. A group of verbs (11)
10. Used to express *to* or *for* in Latin (6)

The term going down the grid is: ....

16 English to Latin crossword

The clues are in English but your answers should be in Latin.

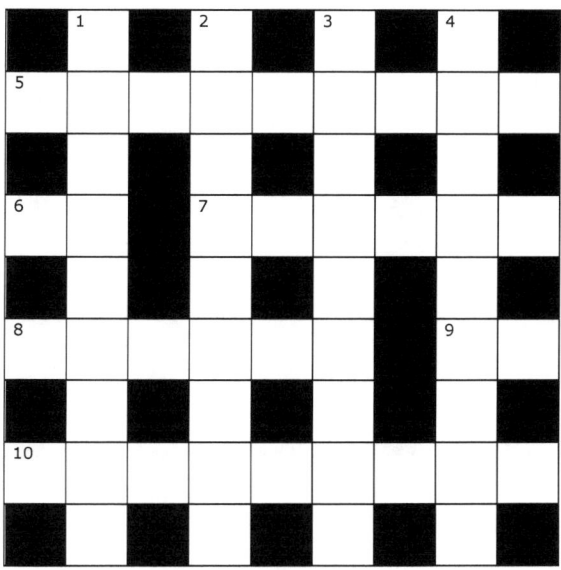

Across

5. Presidents of the games (9)
6. On (2)
7. Of father (6)
8. I terrify (6)
9. Towards (2)
10. Bedroom (9)

Down

1. The horse's reins (5,4)
2. Always for a long time (6,3)
3. Of the dead men (9)
4. Of the women (9)

17   Latin to English crossword

The clues are in Latin but your answers should be in English.

Across

5. difficilis (9)
6. esto (2)
7. audi, age (4,2)
8. pater (6)
9. tam (2)
10. sola, ab (5,4)

Down

1. miser (9)
2. venationis (2,3,4)
3. age somnium (3,1,5)
4. omnes manent (3,2,4)

18 English to Latin crossword

The clues are in English but your answers should be in Latin.

Across

1. O master (6)
4. Who? (4)
7. It is not (3,3)
8. Call! (s) (4)
10. Terrified men (7)
11. On (2)
12. You are (s) (2)
13. Now alone (f) (3,4)
16. For you (s) (4)
17. I live (6)
19. To be (4)
20. They lie (6)

Down

1. They give (4)
2. It remains (5)
3. Us (3)
5. For the wife (5)
6. You (pl) stand (6)
9. For food (4)
11. Angry women (6)
13. You (s) order (5)
14. Act! (pl) (5)
15. After (4)
18. Love! (s) (3)

19   Cryptic Latin crossword

The clues are in English but your answers should be in Latin.

Across

1. They're good in the army (7,4)
7. You should find out (4)
9. You're not out (2,2)
10. He's not taking away (3)
12. Paulina's at home (5)
13. No sun here (5)
15. And don't hang around (2,1)
18. Too big for donkeys (4)
19. A pure, crazy lad (4)
22. They can't see the traffic (7,4)

Down

1. No Roman waters (5,6)
2. Check the book (4)
3. I accuse you (2)
4. Is conditional backward (2)
5. Not some of it (4)
6. Into the politician (2,9)
8. Don't hold on to it (2)
10. Don't fail the test (5)
11. A load of bull (5)
14. What money? (4)
16. And you Brutus? (2)
17. Broken femur in wall (4)
20. O, out you go! (2)
21. A Roman plus (2)

20 Double whammy Latin crossword

The clues are in Latin and your answers should also be in Latin.

Across

6. bonum agis (4)
7. non respondere debes (6)
8. ... Vibius Sabinus (6)
9. non et (3)
11. in equum eo (9)
12. ita vero? nemo dicit. (3)
13. non magistris sed ... (6)
15. puer non est (6)
16. in mare multa est (4)

Down

1. mortui manent in muris ... (11)
2. femina non periculosa (7)
3. Roma est ... (4)
4. non tu (3)
5. non consulibus, sed ... (11)
10. non in taurum (2,5)
13. non sedes (4)
14. triste est. agere debes. (3)

PART 2

Puzzles based on Imperium Latin Book 2

21   Going home

See if you can complete the grid below and by so doing, find out the person whose name goes down the middle of the grid.

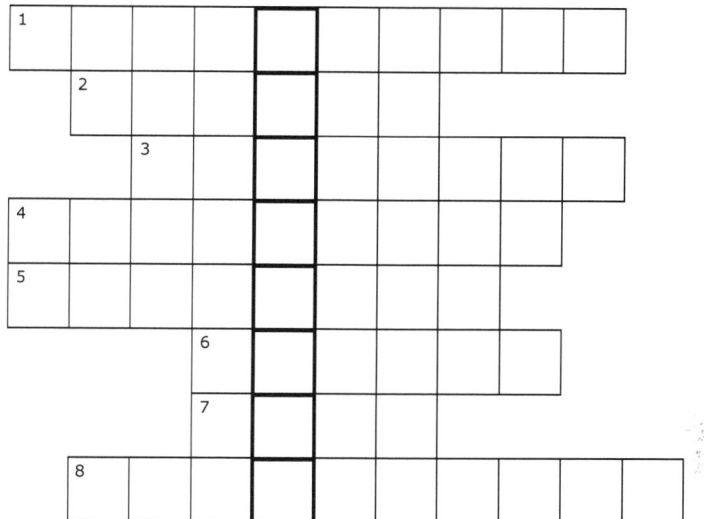

1. He was blinded by a red hot olive pole (10)
2. The goddess who helped Odysseus (6)
3. Helen's husband, who caused the Trojan War (8)
4. The High King of the Greeks at Troy (9)
5. The number one Greek warrior at Troy (8)
6. The name for a going-home myth (6)
7. Homer's style of writing (4)
8. Odysseus' son (10)

The name going down the grid is: ....

22   Homer wordsearch

Find the names and places from the list below, which have all been hidden in the grid.

S	P	O	L	C	Y	C	R	L	A	V	M
F	R	H	D	H	I	M	K	J	G	B	I
M	U	S	E	Y	O	W	R	O	A	N	T
X	A	J	A	Z	S	M	X	I	M	N	E
M	T	E	C	R	E	S	E	A	E	S	L
E	H	S	H	C	I	P	E	R	M	U	E
N	E	R	I	L	L	Y	K	Y	N	M	M
E	N	I	L	G	B	S	O	Q	O	E	A
L	A	F	L	S	O	R	R	H	N	H	C
A	B	Q	E	T	T	S	K	U	K	P	H
U	G	G	S	U	G	R	A	G	I	Y	U
S	C	O	I	T	H	A	C	A	R	L	S
X	N	Y	S	U	E	S	S	Y	D	O	J
A	T	Q	E	P	O	L	E	N	E	P	N

Achilles	epic	Odysseus
Agamemnon	Homer	Odyssey
Ajax	Ithaca	Penelope
Argus	Menelaus	Polyphemus
Athena	Muse	Telemachus
Cyclops	Nostos	Troy

23   Latin to English crossword

The clues are in Latin but your answers should be in English.

Across

4. oculus (3)
6. iratus (5)
7. curre! (3)
8. temperamus (2,7)
10. sunt (3)
13. viae (5)
14. modestus (3)

Down

1. miser (3)
2. eo (1,2)
3. venatoribus (2,7)
5. itis (3,2)
9. terra (5)
11. bellum (3)
12. roga! (3)

24   English to Latin crossword

The clues are in English but your answers should be in Latin.

Across

5. It is written (9)
6. For a good lion (4,5)
7. From an easier thing (9)
8. I look after small things (5,4)

Down

1. I know the house (4,5)
2. I help the men (5,4)
3. I laugh at the joke (5,4)
4. To wound (9)

25 Latin to English crossword

The clues are in Latin but your answers should be in English.

Across

1. respondeat (3,3,5)
5. elephanti (9)
8. in (2)
9. ubi gladiatores pugnant (5)
11. fragor (3)
12. terrae (5)
13. age! (2)
15. narrat puellae (5,4)
17. servi spectant (6,5)

Down

1. neglegit (3,8)
2. oculi (4)
3. curre! (3)
4. ructes (3,3,5)
6. manus (5)
7. gradus (4)
9. et est (3,2)
10. in eo (2,2)
14. donum (4)
16. iace! (3)

26   English to Latin crossword

The clues are in English but your answers should be in Latin.

Across

2. You (s) hold (5)
7. He is silent (5)
8. To stand (5)
10. Of Hannibal's city (11)
12. And (2)
13. Herself (2)
14. Of Odysseus' father (7)
15. From (2)
17. I (acc) (2)
18. Mainz (11)
19. For faith (5)
21. To them you go (3,2)
22. Table (5)

Down

1. She may fall (5)
2. You and health (acc) (2,2,7)
3. And (2)
4. You (s) are (2)
5. I stand in Italy (3,2,6)
6. Of the city (5)
9. Tell! (pl) (7)
10. Dinner (acc) (5)
11. Old man (acc) (5)
16. For the good women (5)
17. With walls (5)
18. That is (abbr) (2)
21. You (s) are (2)

27 Sudoku

You know how Sudoku works. All you have to do is to place numbers one to nine in each vertical and horizontal line and then make sure that each number appears once in each of the nine 3x3 squares. The difference here is that this is Roman Sudoku!

You use the numbers as below:

1	2	3	4	5	6	7	8	9
I	II	III	IV	V	VI	VII	VIII	IX

	IV		I	VII	VI			V
VI	IX		VIII	II				III
		VIII			III			
II			VII	IX				IV
VIII		III				V		VII
IX				V	VIII			II
		VI	V			I		
I				III	IX		V	VI
V			VI	I	IV		VII	

29

28 I'm the man

*The object of the puzzle is to find out which letter of the alphabet is represented by each of the 14 numbers used. You are given two words to start you off, so you can begin by entering any letters from these wherever they appear in the grid. Each word you make should be in good Latin. As you decode each letter, write it in the **Letters deciphered** table and cross it off in the **Letters used** table.*

Letters deciphered

1	2	3	4	5	6	7	8	9	10	11	12	13	14
S	U	M	V	I	R								

Letters used

A	B	D	E	G	I	M	N	O	R	S	T	U	V

29 ArrowWord

All the clues are on the grid. The answers should all be in Latin.

Doesn't know	▼ Reply! (pl)	▼ Rude ones To them ▶					Of the maids	Itself	
▶						These (acc pl) ▶	▼	▼	
You (s) open				Greatly ▼		Lest ▶			
▶									
Of the year									
▶			I press	Don't ▶					
			▼						
You are And		Let me snatch ▶							
▼ ▶									
			Of seas ▶						
But	To whom ▶								

30   A grave challenge

Try to fit all the Latin words into the grid below.

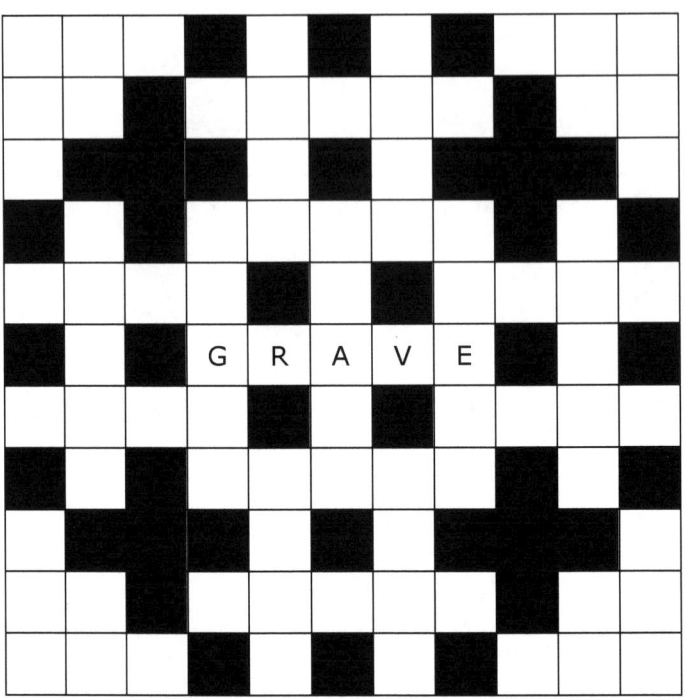

Two letters

da
de
et
it
te
te
ut
ut

Three letters

cui
cur
mei
pax
rem
rex
sed
vis

Four letters

bene
gero
huic
puer
plus
quem
regi
tres

Five letters

aegra
agita
amico
cuius
~~grave~~
irati
opera
rebus
surge
urbes

31   Grammar rules

Grammar is important when you learn Latin, so see if you can fill in the grid and work out what matters most by putting together the letters in the shaded boxes.

Across

2. The action is done to the subject (7)
4. More than (11)
7. Also called final: so that (7)
8. Masculine and Feminine (6)
9. Imperative (7)
12. Needs an antecedent (8)
14. Name of person or thing (4)

Down

1. Indicative or Subjunctive (4)
3. Asking a question (13)
5. Numbers 1 to 3, singular or plural (6)
6. Stands in place of a noun (7)
10. Verbal noun (6)
11. Someone by whom the action is done (5)
13. Active or Passive (5)

It matters most: ....

32   With good reason

Solve the riddle by answering all the statements made below. As you answer each question, insert a letter in the grid below, where you will see two words formed.

Word 1

1.   My first is in epic but not in Circe.
2.   My second is in Odysseus but not in Odyssey.
3.   My third is in Sirens but not in Achilles.
4.   My fourth is in Cyclops and also in nymph.
5.   My fifth is in Troy and also Penelope.
6.   My sixth is a double in suitors and Sirens.
7.   My seventh is in Circe and also Odysseus.

Word 2

1.   My first is in Cyclops and also in Circe.
2.   My second is in Penelope but not in Neptune.
3.   My third is in Calypso but not in Cyclops.
4.   My fourth is in Muse and also in Corfu.
5.   My fifth is in nostos and also in Sirens.
6.   My sixth is in Agamemnon and also in epic.

My whole gives the reason.

1	2	3	4	5	6	7

1	2	3	4	5	6

33   Rome wordsearch

Find the names and places from the list below, which have all been hidden in the grid.

N	H	P	M	U	I	R	T	I	G	S	I
M	S	C	T	E	N	I	T	A	L	A	P
A	U	G	U	S	T	U	S	E	D	F	N
O	N	E	R	O	O	R	C	V	T	A	V
R	Z	J	S	K	G	F	R	R	I	E	E
D	S	R	V	S	A	F	I	V	T	J	S
I	Z	O	R	R	O	U	A	A	U	M	P
N	R	M	U	H	M	L	N	Y	S	N	A
A	E	U	G	K	F	E	O	G	I	I	S
R	M	L	L	U	S	N	O	C	F	B	I
I	U	U	C	E	B	U	N	A	D	N	A
U	S	S	R	E	P	U	B	L	I	C	N
S	R	T	S	U	F	F	E	C	T	S	L
D	O	M	I	T	I	A	N	T	O	G	A

Augustus	Nero	Senate
Colosseum	ordinarius	suffect
consul	Palatine	Titus
Danube	Remus	toga
Domitian	Republic	triumph
Flavian	Romulus	Vespasian

34   Latin to English crossword

The clues are in Latin but your answers should be in English.

Across

6. ferrarii (11)
7. optimum (4)
8. dicit (4)
9. hasta (5)
10. dicimus (2,3)
12. ab (4)
14. rogo (1,3)
15. pompae (11)

Down

1. omnes principes (3,8)
2. seco (1,3)
3. maneo (1,4)
4. sibila (4)
5. mittant (4,3,4)
11. pessimum (5)
13. multum (4)
14. iaceo (1,3)

35 English to Latin crossword

The clues are in English but your answers should be in Latin.

Across

5. We go out (6)
7. Work (4)
8. Rows of seats (7)
9. Them (acc) (3)
11. I may love (4)
13. They may give (4)
15. Hello (3)
17. You (pl) are organised (7)
19. Goodbye (4)
20. You (s) feel (6)

Down

1. Wife (acc) (6)
2. Of all (6)
3. This thing (3)
4. I lead (4)
6. To be hoped (m) (9)
9. They (f) (3)
10. Let it be (3)
11. Love! (s) (3)
12. Organise! (s) (3)
13. For the master (6)
14. It does not happen (3,3)
16. Roads (acc) (4)
18. Lion (3)

36   Why?

Try to fit all the Latin words and phrases into the grid below.

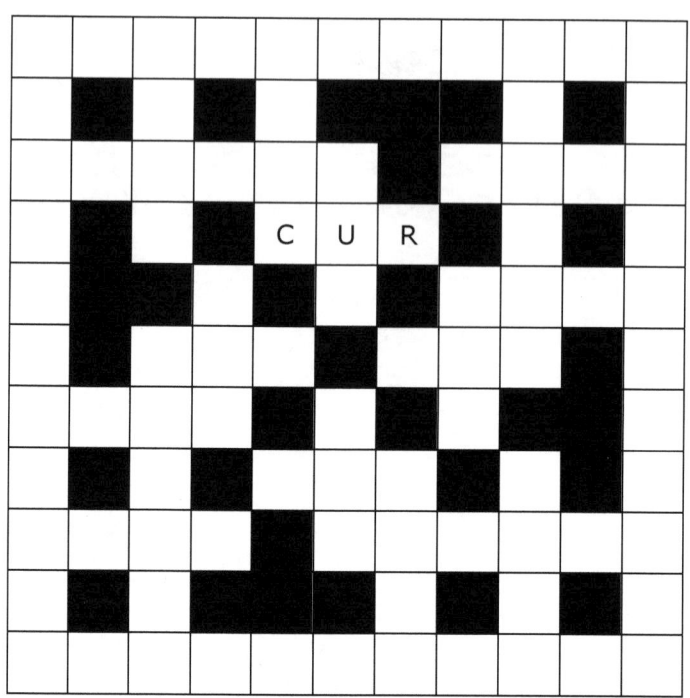

Three letters	**Four letters**	**Six letters**	**Eleven letters**
~~cur~~	aula	audiar	mariti ebrii
fis	ades	reddis	persuadeant
his	deis	rident	pulchriorem
qua	edor	videam	temperamini
sim	hanc		
tua	ludo		
tui	sint		
via	vini		

37   You're falling

*The object of the puzzle is to find out which letter of the alphabet is represented by each of the 18 numbers used. You are given one word to start you off, so you can begin by entering any letters from this wherever they appear in the grid. Each word you make should be in good Latin. As you decode each letter, write it in the **Letters deciphered** table and cross it off in the **Letters used** table.*

Letters deciphered

1	2	3	4	5	6	7	8	9	10	11	12	13	14	15	16	17	18
C	A	D	I	T	S												

Letters used

A	B	C	D	E	G	I	L	M	N	O	P	R	S	T	U	V	X

39

38 Sudoku

You know how Sudoku works. All you have to do is to place numbers one to nine in each vertical and horizontal line and then make sure that each number appears once in each of the nine 3x3 squares. The difference here is that this is Roman Sudoku!

You use the numbers as below:

1	2	3	4	5	6	7	8	9
I	II	III	IV	V	VI	VII	VIII	IX

IV						I		
	VII				VIII	V	IV	
	VIII	I	II					
VII		IV	I	VIII			V	VI
	V		IV	III	IX		VII	
II	I			VI	V	VIII		IV
					IV	VI	II	
	IV	VIII	III				IX	
		V		VII				VIII

39   Latin to English crossword

The clues are in Latin but your answers should be in English.

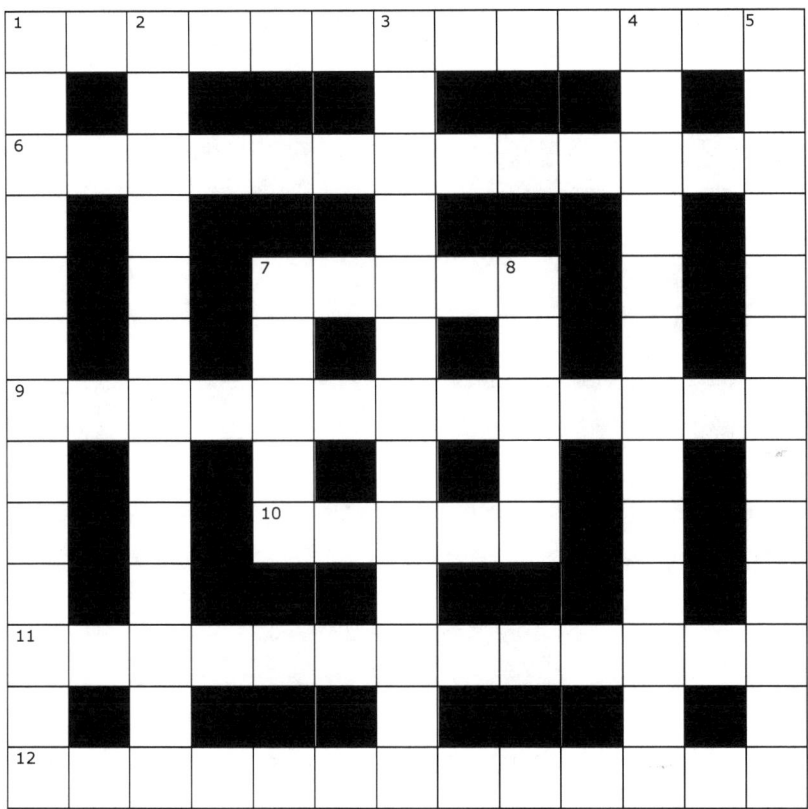

Across

1. optimus in arena (4,9)
6. procedat (3,3,7)
7. naves (5)
9. clamandi (2,3,8)
10. consilia (5)
11. ita audio fabulam (2,1,4,1,5)
12. ad tuas vias (2,4,7)

Down

1. ludo sedere (2,6,2,3)
2. terreat (3,3,7)
3. loci ubi arenae sint (13)
4. navigant soli (4,4,5)
5. scurriles irati oculi (4,5,4)
7. dormite (5)
8. limaces (5)

40   English to Latin crossword

The clues are in English but your answers should be in Latin.

Across

7. Where the arena was (13)
8. For the lion (5)
11. I learn (5)
12. She may invite (7)
13. With hope (3)
14. To go (3)
15. Soldiers (7)
16. A man (3)
17. Heart (3)
18. We fall (7)
20. He may know (5)
21. A radish (5)
24. For the spectators (13)

Down

1. All for the emperor (5,8)
2. Of the Rhine (5)
3. Go! (pl) (3)
4. You (s) may give (3)
5. And it happens (2,3)
6. For the more beautiful (13)
9. She invites (7)
10. Manly (7)
11. We are destroyed (7)
18. Of a blind man (5)
19. With rocks (5)
22. Them (f acc) (3)
23. Night (3)

PART 3

Puzzles based on Imperium Latin Book 3

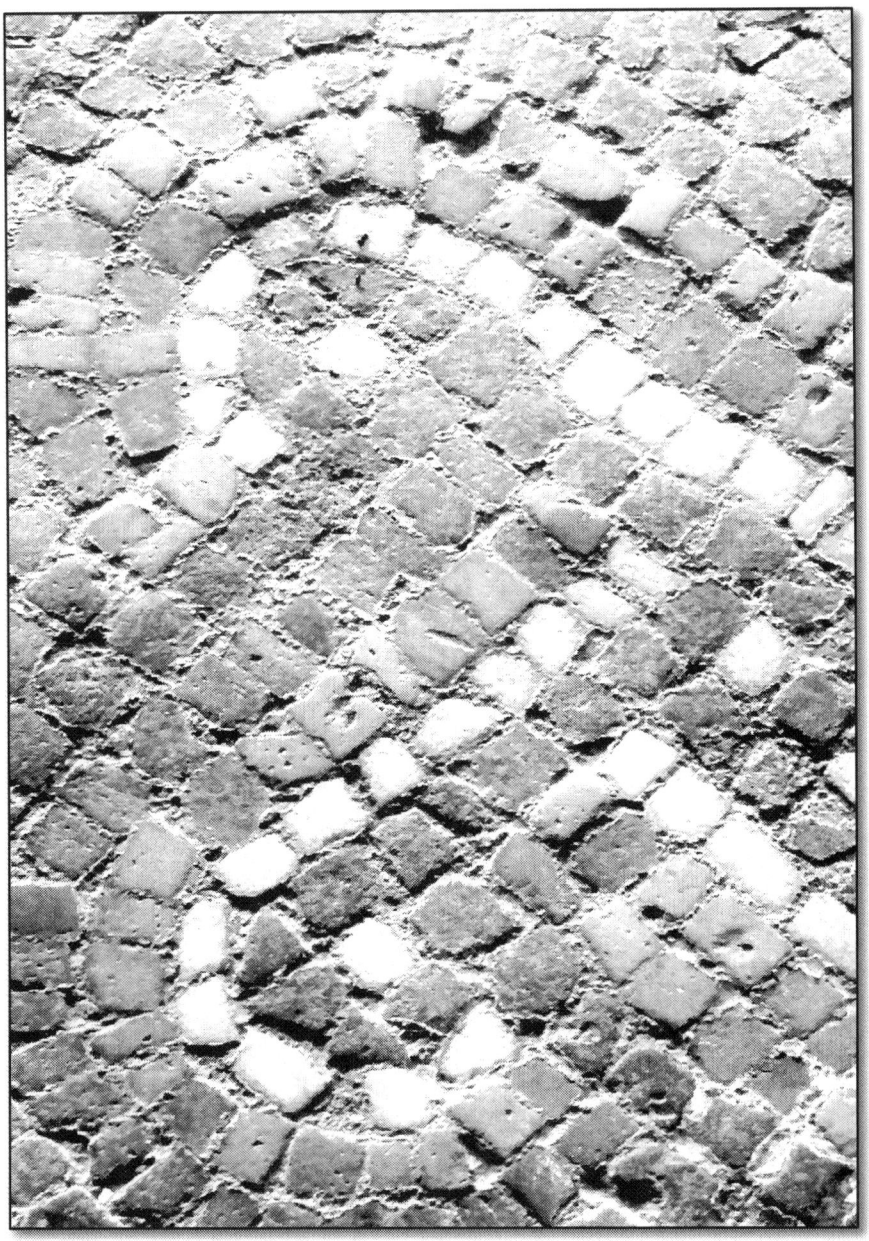

41   Hadrian's places

See if you can complete the grid below and by so doing, find out the place name which goes down the middle of it.

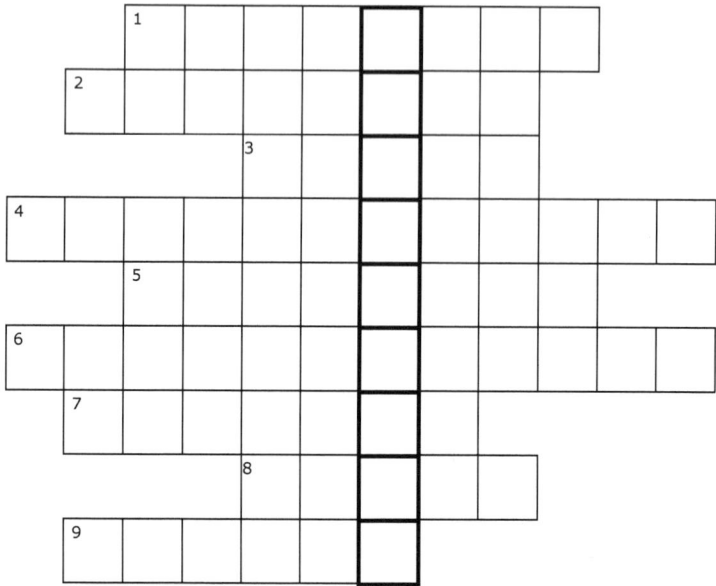

1. The Latin name of where Hadrian was first posted to as military tribune (8)
2. The name for the line of stones in Rome, indicating the extent of the city (8)
3. The kingdom of Decebalus (5)
4. The city which was built to commemorate Antinous (12)
5. The English name of 1 (8)
6. Bithynium ......, where Hadrian met Antinous (12)
7. Where Hadrian died (7)
8. Hadrian was posted here to serve as military tribune under Servianus (5)
9. Hadrian became Archon here (6)

The place name going down the grid is: ....

42   Latin Verbs-only crossword

The clues are in English but your answers should be in Latin.

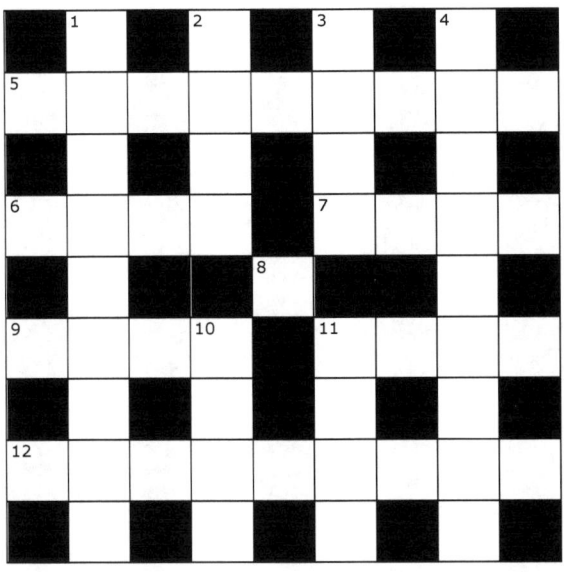

Across

5. They had had (9)
6. Let it stand (4)
7. I will have gone (4)
8. Go! (s) (1)
9. To be (4)
11. I will give (4)
12. They might send (9)

Down

1. I may have been captured (9)
2. He has been (4)
3. I urged (4)
4. They were entering (9)
10. Be! (s) (4)
11. To be given (4)

43 They know I'm first

Try to fit all the Latin words and phrases into the grid below.

S	C	I	O	R	P	R	I	M	U	S

Three letters

avi
sic
sit
sta
sua
sum
tot
via

Eleven letters

amavissetis
collata sint
gladiatores
magistrorum
multa egisti
praetoribus
~~scior primus~~
visitabimus

44   Who's at the door?

Martial has lots of friends but only one of them is at the door asking for him right now. Fill in the grid and work out who this is by putting together the letters in the shaded boxes.

Across

4. He's a doctor with 100 students (9)
6. His first name is Safronius and he's asking about girls (5)
8. She's a flower arranger (5)
9. He needs to pay up quick or he'll end up in court (6)
11. She won't write back but maybe she'll pay in another way (6)
13. Nobody should lend money to this chap (5)
14. He's keen to marry old ladies who might die (8)
15. He's promising to give Martial money but only when he dies (4)

Down

1. She carries away her girlfriends (7)
2. He writes 200 lines of verse every day (5)
3. He won't promise or refuse quickly enough (5)
5. He's surprised at the cost of a mule driver (5)
7. She has very large breasts (8)
10. He buys so many things he'll soon run out of money (6)
12. He's too sober to make a proper friend (4)

The friend at the door is: ....

45   Martial's mates

Solve the riddle by answering all the statements made below. As you answer each question, insert a letter in the grid below, where you will see two words formed.

Word 1

1.   My first is in Aper and also in Avitus.
2.   My second is in Maro and twice in Mamercus.
3.   My third is in Linus and also in Thais.
4.   My fourth is in Cinna and also in Castor.
5.   My fifth comes twice in Aemilianus and also in Caedicianus.

Word 2

1.   My first is in Polla but not in Paula.
2.   My second is in Aemilianus but not Saleianus.
3.   My third is Linus and doubles in Cinna.
4.   My fourth is in Cerylus but not in Lycoris.
5.   My fifth is in Paulus but not in Paula.

Word 3

1.   My first is in Varus and also in Thais.
2.   My second is in Linus but not in Lycoris.
3.   My third is Cinna but not in Atticus.
4.   My fourth is in Castor but not in Maro.

My whole tells the tale.

46   Campaigns and Politics wordsearch

Find the names and places from the list below, which have all been hidden in the grid.

N	S	U	C	S	U	F	S	J	L	O	P
E	U	F	T	A	D	I	U	T	R	I	X
R	I	V	N	R	A	S	L	R	S	R	R
V	L	W	O	M	C	E	A	A	U	K	L
A	E	D	I	I	I	R	B	I	N	U	S
C	N	A	G	Z	A	V	E	A	A	A	U
E	R	M	E	E	N	I	C	N	I	Q	N
B	O	N	L	G	X	A	E	U	R	U	A
U	C	A	Q	E	Z	N	D	S	D	I	I
N	C	T	B	T	L	U	S	U	A	N	T
A	V	I	N	H	M	S	K	S	H	C	I
D	M	O	G	U	N	T	I	A	C	U	M
F	Z	O	E	S	C	U	S	K	P	M	O
R	E	G	I	A	S	U	C	I	C	A	D

Adiutrix	damnatio	Moguntiacum
Aquincum	Danube	Nerva
Cornelius	Decebalus	Oescus
Fuscus	Domitianus	Sarmizegethusa
Dacian	Hadrianus	Servianus
Dacicus	Legion	Traianus

47   Latin to English crossword

The clues are in Latin but your answers should be in English.

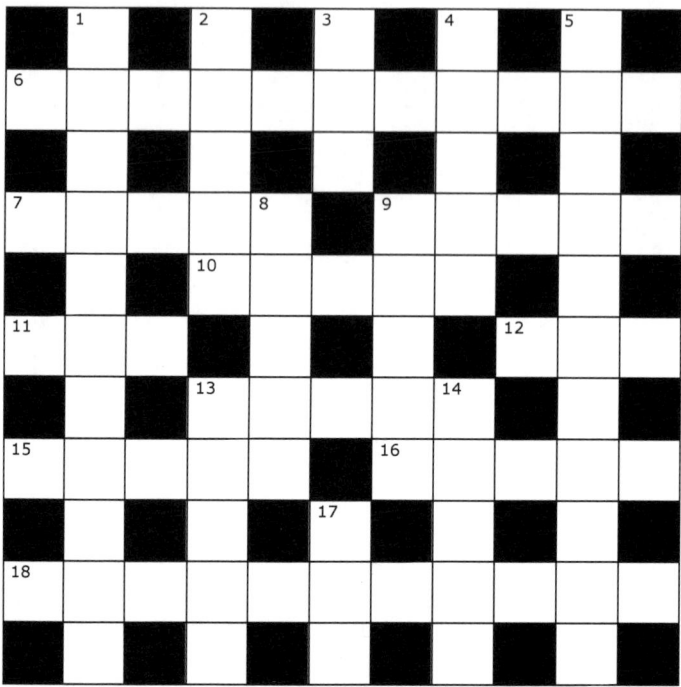

Across

6. ille ambulaverat (2,3,6)
7. pugna (5)
9. ira (5)
10. naves (5)
11. aeger (3)
12. explorator (3)
13. sunt in (3,2)
15. debere (2,3)
16. aquilo (pars una) (5)
18. bonus senex (1,4,3,3)

Down

1. tussiemus (2,4,5)
2. thermae (5)
3. duo (3)
4. consilia (5)
5. ille iuvat Troiam (2,5,4)
8. ibi (5)
9. taedium (1,4)
13. silva (1,4)
14. minime, ago (2,1,2)
17. filius (3)

48 It's here

*The object of the puzzle is to find out which letter of the alphabet is represented by each of the 17 numbers used. You are given one word to start you off, so you can begin by entering any letters from this wherever they appear in the grid. Each word you make should be in good Latin. As you decode each letter, write it in the **Letters deciphered** table and cross it off in the **Letters used** table.*

1 A	2 D	3 E	4 S	5 T	■	9	1	15	9	1
15	■	12	■	3	■	11	■	3	■	2
11	14	17	3	15	1	9	1	5	11	4
2	■	7	■	15	■	11	■	11	■	11
1	14	11	13	1	■	4	3	16	3	14
■	■	13	■	■	■	■	■	3	■	■
1	14	1	5	1	■	13	11	9	10	14
8	■	16	■	7	■	1	■	1	■	11
15	3	2	11	11	4	4	3	14	10	4
6	■	10	■	10	■	5	■	10	■	13
4	11	14	10	4	■	11	11	4	4	3

Letters deciphered

1	2	3	4	5	6	7	8	9	10	11	12	13	14	15	16	17
A	D	E	S	T												

Letters used

A	B	C	D	E	G	I	L	M	N	O	P	R	S	T	U	X

49   Sudoku

You know how Sudoku works. All you have to do is to place numbers one to nine in each vertical and horizontal line and then make sure that each number appears once in each of the nine 3x3 squares. The difference here is that this is Roman Sudoku!

You use the numbers as below:

1	2	3	4	5	6	7	8	9
I	II	III	IV	V	VI	VII	VIII	IX

VIII			III			IV	V	VII
	IX	I			VII	II		VIII
	III		II			I		
I				VIII		VI	II	
	VIII	IX		I	VII			
	IV	V		VI				I
	II				VI		I	
VI		III				V	VII	
IV	I	VII			III			II

50   ArrowWord

All the clues are on the grid. The answers should all be in Latin.

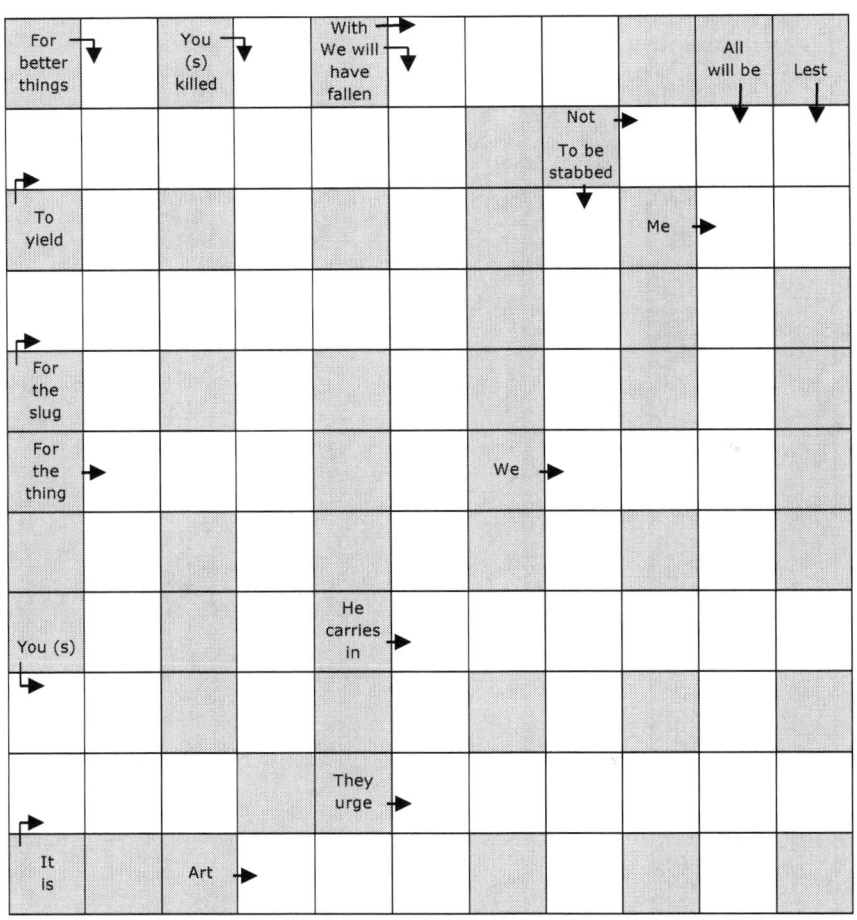

51   Latin to English crossword

The clues are in Latin but your answers should be in English.

1		2		3		4		5		6

Across

1. ludis (4,7)
7. adeo (2)
8. vendit (5)
9. is (2)
12. carnifex (11)
13. rerum publicarum (2,9)
14. minime (2)
15. age id (3,2)
16. in (2)
19. transimus tempora (2,4,5)

Down

1. nos te iam videmus (2,3,3,3)
2. ad (2)
3. suspicit (3,8)
4. aula aedificata est (4,2,5)
5. in (2)
6. praebet (3,8)
10. lacrimae (5)
11. fragore (2,3)
17. non sub (2)
18. sum (2)

52   English to Latin crossword
The clues are in English but your answers should be in Latin.

Across

5. You (s) might have founded (11)
8. You (s) are (2)
9. It stands (4)
10. She has gone away (5)
12. I am (3)
14. 49 (2)
15. Let me rule (5)
17. If (2)
18. For (3)
20. I travel (5)
22. I played (4)
23. I give (2)
24. I might have been a broken woman (6,5)

Down

1. I will have demanded (11)
2. You (s) may be (3)
3. To him (2)
4. I might have been ruled (6,5)
6. Let it be given (5)
7. Of themselves (3)
10. Rampart (5)
11. You (s) go (2)
13. To me (shortened) (2)
14. Non ex (2)
16. Bad men (acc) (5)
19. Not you (2)
21. To this place (3)
23. She may give (3)
25. You (acc) (2)

53   All done

Try to fit all the Latin words and phrases into the grid below.

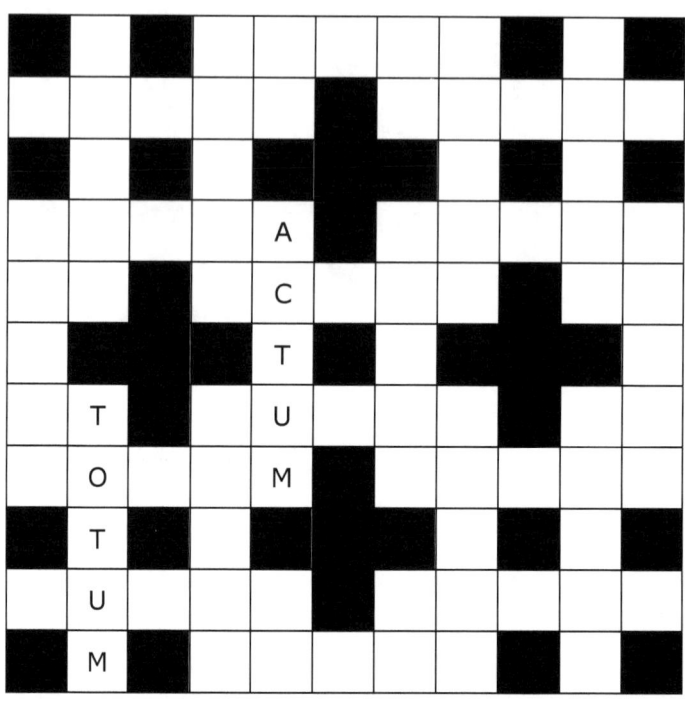

Two letters

ab
da
ea
ei
it
si
tu
vi

Five letters

~~actum~~
addis
aegra
arida
cervi
credo
ducis
ebrii

erasi
esset
facis
fuero
infer
intro
oculo
olere

opera
orare
orbes
simus
solam
spera
teneo
~~totum~~

54   Sudoku

You know how Sudoku works. All you have to do is to place numbers one to nine in each vertical and horizontal line and then make sure that each number appears once in each of the nine 3x3 squares. The difference here is that this is Roman Sudoku!

You use the numbers as below:

1	2	3	4	5	6	7	8	9
I	II	III	IV	V	VI	VII	VIII	IX

IV	VI			V	III	II		
III	I				VI			
			I	IX				VI
		I		VII	II	VIII		III
VII	III						I	II
II		VIII	IV	III		V		
I				VI	V			
			VII				II	IV
		VI	IX	II			III	V

55   Martial wordsearch

Find the names of Martial's friends in the grid, which have all been taken from the list below and mixed up to confuse you.

G	C	F	A	C	O	R	D	U	S	U	R
M	A	T	Q	B	S	Z	E	D	X	U	H
A	E	L	R	P	A	U	L	A	F	H	V
R	Y	H	L	J	S	S	L	U	O	L	P
O	E	S	D	A	S	A	S	W	L	Q	H
D	S	U	R	A	V	A	F	A	K	L	I
S	C	C	R	E	T	T	B	I	B	M	L
U	Z	C	T	R	T	H	A	I	S	G	E
M	D	A	S	I	U	S	N	S	N	S	R
U	E	L	N	O	R	T	A	S	Y	U	O
T	W	F	R	N	W	V	E	R	E	L	S
S	H	T	Q	U	I	E	V	A	R	U	T
O	J	R	G	S	U	C	I	T	T	A	D
P	R	I	S	C	U	S	A	R	F	K	E

Atticus	Flaccus	Postumus
Aulus	Galla	Priscus
Bassa	Maro	Rufus
Cinna	Naevia	Sabinus
Cordus	Paula	Thais
Dasius	Phileros	Varus

56   They'll love it

*The object of the puzzle is to find out which letter of the alphabet is represented by each of the 18 numbers used. You are given two words to start you off, so you can begin by entering any letters from these wherever they appear in the grid. Each word you make should be in good Latin. As you decode each letter, write it in the **Letters deciphered** table and cross it off in the **Letters used** table.*

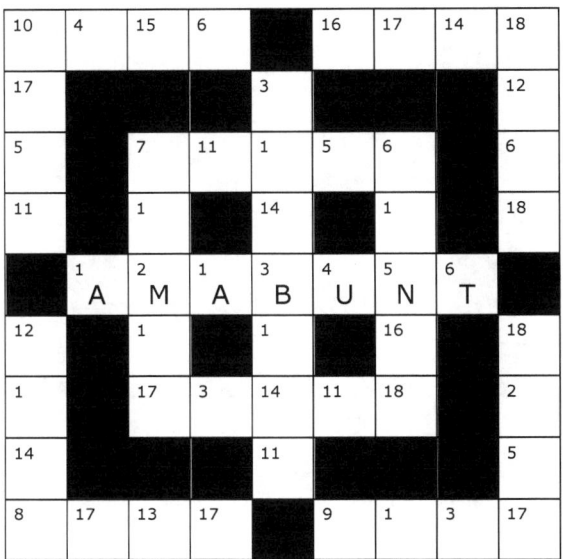

Letters deciphered

1	2	3	4	5	6	7	8	9	10	11	12	13	14	15	16	17	18
A	M	B	U	N	T												

Letters used

A	B	D	E	F	G	H	I	L	M	N	O	P	R	S	T	U	V

57 Latin to English crossword

The clues are in Latin but your answers should be in English.

Across

7. patiemini (3,4,6)
8. hoc (4)
9. sede (3)
10. tempus (4)
11. id (2)
12. tam (2)
14. Ovidii (5)
17. Boreas sine vento (5)
19. et (3)
20. canto (1,4)
22. doce (5)
23. leonis sine leo (2)
25. age (2)
26. castra (4)
28. securis (3)
29. fama (4)
30. voluimus sedere (2,6,2,3)

Down

1. mansistis (3,4,6)
2. debet (4)
3. perdidi (1,4)
4. est eius (2,3)
5. eius (2,2)
6. videtur committere (5,2,6)
11. est (2)
13. in (2)
15. fragor (3)
16. ulli (3)
18. unum (3)
21. ite! (2)
22. ad (2)
24. fides (5)
25. facta (5)
27. ludo (4)
29. fluo (4)

58   English to Latin crossword

The clues are in English but your answers should be in Latin.

Across

7. We had greeted (13)
8. Part (4)
9. Lion (3)
10. With fire (4)
11. Around (6)
13. I carry towards (6)
15. Bull (acc) (6)
17. You (pl) must create! (6)
18. For you (s) (4)
20. Man (3)
21. Bear (4)
22. It's for authors (10,3)

Down

1. With calamities (13)
2. Whom (acc m pl) (4)
3. Sky (6)
4. Recall! (s) (6)
5. For the dog (4)
6. He's wounded (10,3)
12. Why (3)
14. Weep! (s) (3)
16. To move (6)
17. I will look after (6)
19. That awful man (4)
21. I urged (4)

59   Latin to English crossword

The clues are in Latin but your answers should be in English.

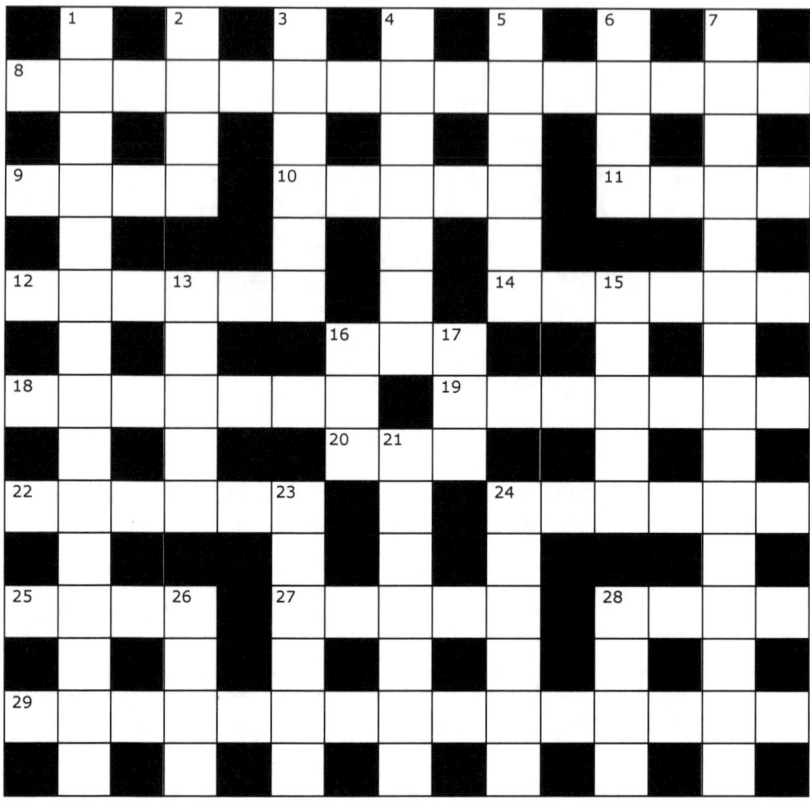

Across

8. ille possit esse (2,3,2,4,2,2)
9. feles (4)
10. egredior (5)
11. taedium (4)
12. perite! (6)
14. senatus (6)
16. cinis (3)
18. relinque! (7)
19. videtur (2,5)
20. egi sine me (3)
22. rapi! (6)
24. negamus (2,4)
25. sepulcrum (4)
27. mensis (5)
28. domum (4)
29. is nolebat (2,3,3,7)

Down

1. reliquimus (2,4,9)
2. dies (4)
3. ructo (1,5)
4. palatia (7)
5. classes (6)
6. gradus (4)
7. aedificavi monumentum (1,5,1,8)
13. non est (2,3)
15. nullus finis (2,3)
16. et (3)
17. celavit (3)
21. dono (1,6)
23. homines (6)
24. audimus (2,4)
26. ursa (4)
28. odi sine me (4)

60 Double whammy Latin crossword

The clues are in Latin and your answers should also be in Latin.

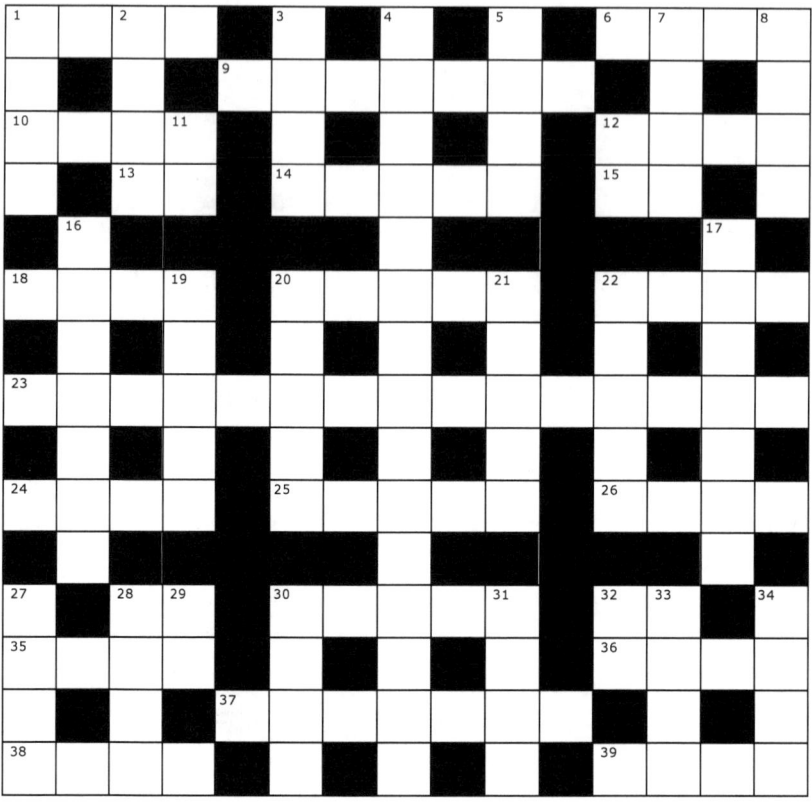

Across

1. nullus homo (4)
6. ille mei est (4)
9. non dixi - carmen erat (7)
10. quale? (4)
12. quod adiutrici dicis (4)
13. quis? (2)
14. in fluminibus vides (5)
15. donum a me (2)
18. die? mense? minime! (4)
20. usque nunc (2,3)
22. ubi pisces natant (4)
23. principem adiuvabant (10,5)
24. eo (4)
25. non laeto sed ... (5)
26. amicos mei (4)
28. quid? (2)
30. quibus equum temperas (5)
32. non venio (2)
35. maria (4)
36. quae speras (4)
37. affert? minime! heri fecit. (7)
38. promitto? gravius est. (4)
39. esse debetis (4)

Down

1. non ignota est (4)
2. non boni sunt (4)
3. villa (4)
4. caput in arena ponit (15)
5. Polyphemus tale animal habuit (4)
7. non asino sed ... (4)
8. puellae sui (4)
11. inter sum et est (2)
12. nec is nec ea (2)
16. quae vagula erat (7)
17. rumpor (7)
19. amabo? minime! (5)
20. mihi multum placuerunt (5)
21. donum meum accipit (3,2)
22. vinum sine aqua (5)
27. aquae et ... (4)
28. via (4)
29. dare debes (2)
30. mors (4)
31. appropinquat (4)
32. vivis (2)
33. labor (4)
34. esse aut non? (4)

SOLUTIONS

1 Meet the folks

```
    P A U L I N A
  A E L I U S
    D O M I T I A
  M A T I D I A
U L P I U S
  A N N A
    A F E R
```

The answer: Plotina

2 Names wordsearch

E	R	R	D	N	I	T	A	L	I	C	A
F	E	U	O	C	Y	J	L	X	M	N	E
W	F	C	M	A	T	I	D	I	A	V	M
A	A	W	I	D	S	T	S	Q	R	H	O
P	L	O	T	I	N	A	I	D	C	T	R
B	T	G	I	Z	P	L	I	Z	U	N	G
A	T	R	A	A	N	I	B	A	S	Q	E
I	G	A	P	E	D	C	W	F	R	U	N
N	L	E	A	R	I	U	S	E	T	A	S
A	E	C	U	B	L	I	E	D	I	E	T
P	R	U	L	P	U	N	T	R	R	L	I
S	A	L	I	Q	A	E	D	O	N	I	A
I	R	U	N	A	J	A	R	T	H	U	R
H	S	S	A	T	H	V	W	E	W	S	T

3 English to Latin crossword

```
D U O ■ E S T I S
U ■ ■ ■ X ■ E ■ U
C A S A S ■ R ■ M
I ■ ■ ■ P ■ R ■ ■
T E M P E R A R E
■ ■ O ■ C ■ ■ ■ ■
S ■ V ■ T I M E S
E ■ E ■ A ■ ■ ■ T
D A T I S ■ E G O
```

4 Sudoku

II	VI	V	VIII	III	IV	IX	VII	I
IX	III	VIII	I	II	VII	V	IV	VI
VII	IV	I	IX	V	VI	III	VIII	II
III	IX	VII	VI	VIII	I	II	V	IV
I	V	VI	IV	VII	II	VIII	IX	III
IV	VIII	II	V	IX	III	I	VI	VII
VI	I	IX	III	IV	VIII	VII	II	V
VIII	VII	III	II	VI	V	IV	I	IX
V	II	IV	VII	I	IX	VI	III	VIII

5 Sadly I sit

```
■ C ■ V I A ■ S ■
N O N ■ N ■ C U R
■ R ■ M ■ V ■ M ■
S ■ F I L I A ■ E
T U ■ S ■ D ■ E S
O ■ S E D E O ■ T
■ T ■ R ■ O ■ N ■
I A M ■ D ■ V O S
■ M ■ V O X ■ S ■
```

6 English to Latin crossword

```
■ ■ F ■ I ■ S ■ ■
C E L E R I T E R
U ■ E ■ E ■ A ■ O
I R A T A ■ E T E G O
T ■ E ■ T ■ E ■ O
I A M ■ D A T ■ N O S
U ■ S ■ M ■ A ■ M
U R B E S ■ A G U N T
U ■ L ■ V ■ R ■ I
S O L L I C I T A
■ A ■ A ■ S ■ ■
```

7 Latin to English crossword

A		H			B	M		D
F	I	E	L	D	Y	O	U	D	O
T		A			U		S		W
E	A	R	T	H	S	I	T	I	N
R		T	O		U		A		
	A		A	D	O	O	R		M
	S		L		G	O			W
I	K	I	L	L	S	E	R	V	E
N		A		E		D			A
T	O	S	E	A	I	H	E	A	R
O		K		D		R			E

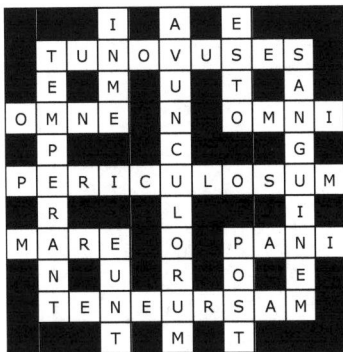

10 English to Latin crossword

		I		A		E		
	T	U	N	O	V	U	S	E	S
	E		M		U		T		A
O	M	N	E		N		O	M	N	I
	P			C			G	
P	E	R	I	C	U	L	O	S	U	M
	R			L			I	
M	A	R	E		O		P	A	N	I
	N		U		R		O		E
T	E	N	E	U	R	S	A	M
	T		M		T

8 Spanish connections

	C	A	R	T	H	A	G	E
		C	A	P	U	A
S	A	R	D	I	N	I	A
	A	L	C	A	N	T	A	R	A
	C	O	R	S	I	C	A
H	A	S	D	R	U	B	A	L
		T	A	G	U	S
	S	I	C	I	L	Y

The answer: Hannibal

11 Latin to English crossword

B	O	A	R	S		B	U	L	L	S
L		N				E		O
O	R	D	E	R	S	B	E	A	R	S
O		W			R		A
D		E	A	T	S	O	N	D
	P			T
T		L	I	E	I	G	O	B
I		E			L	R
R	O	A	D	S	W	E	L	O	V	E
E		S			V	A
D	R	E	A	M	I	S	E	N	D

9 ArrowWord

	I		E		S	E	D	
Q	U	O	Q	U	E		I	R	E
	B		U		N		I	E	X
F	E	M	I	N	A		N		S
	M		C		T		T	P
U	B	I		O		E	G	O
	S		B		R		L	N
	V		U		I	N	L	U	D	O
D	O		S		B		E	E
E	S	T		U	R	G	E	R	E
		D	A	S		O	E

12 We hear the waters

A	U	D	I		M	A	R	E
M		A			S
A		A	N	N	A	E	S
T		Q		C	Q	E
	A	U	D	I	M	U	S
Q		A	L	I	A
U	S	O	L	U	S	P
O		A	R
D	E	B	E	N	O	L	I

13 Sudoku

II	IV	I	III	V	VI	VII	IX	VIII
VIII	IX	VII	II	I	IV	VI	III	V
V	VI	III	IX	VII	VIII	IV	I	II
IV	III	V	VIII	VI	VII	I	II	IX
VII	I	II	IV	III	IX	VIII	V	VI
VI	VIII	IX	I	II	V	III	IV	VII
I	VII	VIII	V	IV	II	IX	VI	III
IX	II	IV	VI	VIII	III	V	VII	I
III	V	VI	VII	IX	I	II	VIII	IV

14 Politics and History wordsearch

V	I	A	A	P	P	I	A	N	R	G	H
I	C	H	A	N	N	I	B	A	L	L	D
C	P	A	N	V	U	R	O	A	D	A	R
Z	R	L	C	F	R	V	R	I	B	D	O
E	O	U	T	A	E	E	K	R	I	W	
N	V	G	V	A	R	E	N	A	N	A	S
U	I	I	W	Y	G	T	J	C	K	T	N
T	N	L	T	R	L	I	H	Z	V	O	E
P	C	A	L	I	G	I	L	A	I	R	D
E	E	C	Q	E	Y	N	C	H	G	R	O
N	X	D	M	V	M	W	O	I	R	E	O
O	A	T	I	H	L	L	O	R	S	Z	W
C	O	L	O	S	S	E	U	M	J	F	F
I	B	V	V	E	S	P	A	S	I	A	N

15 Not so polite

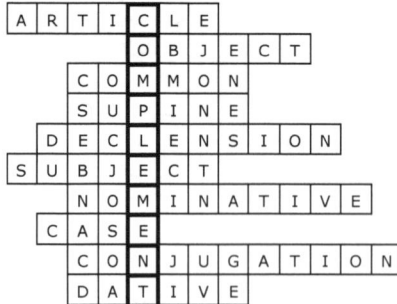

The answer: Complement

16 English to Latin crossword

	F		S		M		F	
P	R	A	E	T	O	R	E	S
	E		M		R		M	
I	N		P	A	T	R	I	S
	A		E		U		N	
T	E	R	R	E	O		A	D
	Q		D		R		R	
C	U	B	I	C	U	L	U	M
	I		U		M		M	

17 Latin to English crossword

	M		O		A		A	
D	I	F	F	I	C	U	L	T
	S		T		T		L	
B	E		H	E	A	R	D	O
	R		E		D		O	
F	A	T	H	E	R		S	O
	B		U		E		T	
A	L	O	N	E	A	W	A	Y
	E		T		M		Y	

18 English to Latin crossword

D	O	M	I	N	E		Q	U	I	S
A		A		O				X		T
N	O	N	E	S	T		V	O	C	A
T		E				C		R		T
		T	E	R	R	I	T	I		I
I	N			O		B			E	S
R		I	A	M	S	O	L	A		
A		U		A				G		P
T	I	B	I		H	A	B	I	T	O
A		E				M		T		S
E	S	S	E		I	A	C	E	N	T

19 Cryptic Latin crossword

M	I	L	I	T	E	S	B	O	N	I
A		E		E		I		M		N
R	O	G	A		D		I	N	E	S
I		E	D	A	T		E		E	
A			I		A				N	
G	A	D	E	S		U	M	B	R	A
R			C		R				T	
A		Q	E	T	I		M		O	
E	Q	U	I		E		P	U	E	R
C		I	T		E		R		E	
A	U	D	I	U	N	T	V	I	A	M

20 Double whammy Latin crossword

	S		B		U		E		P	
B	E	N	E		R	O	G	A	R	E
	P		N		B		O		A	
L	U	C	I	U	S			S	E	D
	L		G				I		T	
	C	O	N	S	C	E	N	D	O	
	R		A				U		R	
N	O	N			S	E	R	V	I	S
	R		F		T		S		B	
P	U	E	L	L	A		A	Q	U	A
	M		E		S		M		S	

21 Going home

P	O	L	Y	P	H	E	M	U	S	
	A	T	H	E	N	A				
		M	E	N	E	L	A	U	S	
A	G	A	M	E	M	N	O	N		
A	C	H	I	L	L	E	S			
			N	O	S	T	O	S		
			E	P	I	C				
	T	E	L	E	M	A	C	H	U	S

The answer: Penelope

22 Homer wordsearch

S	P	O	L	C	Y	C	R	L	A	V	M
F	R	H	D	H	I	M	K	J	G	B	I
M	U	S	E	Y	O	W	R	O	A	N	T
X	A	J	A	Z	S	M	X	I	M	N	E
M	T	E	C	R	E	S	E	A	E	S	L
E	H	S	H	C	I	P	E	R	M	U	E
N	E	R	I	L	L	Y	K	Y	N	M	M
E	N	I	L	G	B	S	O	Q	O	E	A
L	A	F	L	S	O	R	R	H	N	H	C
A	B	Q	E	T	T	S	K	U	K	P	H
U	G	G	S	U	G	R	A	G	I	Y	U
S	C	O	I	T	H	A	C	A	R	L	S
X	N	Y	S	U	E	S	S	Y	D	O	J
A	T	Q	E	P	O	L	E	N	E	P	N

23 Latin to English crossword

S		I		B		E	Y	E
A	N	G	R	Y			O	
D		O		H		R	U	N
				U			G	
W	E	C	O	N	T	R	O	L
	A			T				
A	R	E		E		W		A
	T			R	O	A	D	S
S	H	Y		S		R		K

24 English to Latin crossword

	S		V		R		V	
S	C	R	I	B	I	T	U	R
	I		R		D		L	
B	O	N	O	L	E	O	N	I
	C		S		O		E	
F	A	C	I	L	I	O	R	E
	S		U		O		A	
P	A	R	V	A	C	U	R	O
	M		O		O		E	

25 Latin to English crossword

```
S H E M A Y R E P L Y
H   Y         U     O
E L E P H A N T S   U
N   S   A       T   M
E     O N   A R E N A
G   I   D I N   P   Y
L A N D S   D O     B
E   I       I   G   E
C   T E L L S G I R L
T       I       F   C
S L A V E S W A T C H
```

26 English to Latin crossword

```
  C   T E N E S   U
T A C E T   S T A R E
  D   E   N   O   B
C A R T H A G I N I S
E T   S   R   N   S E
N   L A E R T I S   N
A B   L   A   T   M E
M O G U N T I A C U M
  N   T   E   L   R
F I D E I   E I S I S
  S   M E N S A   S
```

27 Sudoku

III	IV	II	I	VII	VI	IX	VIII	V
VI	IX	I	VIII	II	V	VII	IV	III
VII	V	VIII	IX	IV	III	II	VI	I
II	VI	V	VII	IX	I	VIII	III	IV
VIII	I	III	IV	VI	II	V	IX	VII
IX	VII	IV	III	V	VIII	VI	I	II
IV	III	VI	V	VIII	VII	I	II	IX
I	VIII	VII	II	III	IX	IV	V	VI
V	II	IX	VI	I	IV	III	VII	VIII

28 I'm the man

```
    T   B   S
  A U D I R I S
A B I   B   M E O
  E   R E I   D
E S S E   A G E R
  T   S U M   T
V I R   N   S I S
  S E N A T U S
    S   M   I
```

29 ArrowWord

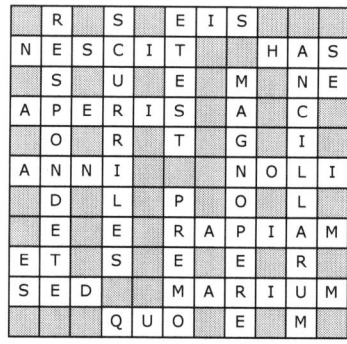

```
  R   S   E I S
N E S C I T     H A S
  S   U   E   M   N E
A P E R I S   A   C
  O   R   T   G   I
A N N I       N O L I
  D   L   P   O   L
  E   E   R A P I A M
E T   S   E   E   R
S E D     M A R I U M
      Q U O   E   M
```

30 A grave challenge

```
C U I   Q   H   V I S
U T   C U I U S   T E
R       E   I       D
  R   A M I C O   S
B E N E   R   P L U S
  B   G R A V E   R
P U E R   T   R E G I
  S   A G I T A   E
R       E   R       R
E T   U R B E S   D E
M E I   O   S   P A X
```

31 Grammar rules

	M		P	A	S	S	I	V	E		
	O					N					
C	O	M	P	A	R	A	T	I	V	E	
	D		E			E					
P			R		P	U	R	P	O	S	E
R			S			R					
C	O	M	M	O	N		C	O	M	M	A	N	D
N			N		G		G				
O		A		R	E	L	A	T	I	V	E
U		G			R		T			O	
N		E			U		I			I	
	N	O	U	N		V		C	
		T			D		E			E	

The answer: Superlative

32 With good reason

| P | U | R | P | O | S | E | | C | L | A | U | S | E |

33 Rome wordsearch

N	H	P	M	U	I	R	T	I	G	S	I
M	S	C	T	E	N	I	T	A	L	A	P
A	U	G	U	S	T	U	S	E	D	F	N
O	N	E	R	O	O	R	C	V	T	A	V
R	Z	J	S	K	G	F	R	R	I	E	E
D	S	R	V	S	A	F	I	V	T	J	S
I	Z	O	R	R	O	U	A	A	U	M	P
N	R	M	U	H	M	L	N	Y	S	N	A
A	E	U	G	K	F	E	O	G	I	I	S
R	M	L	L	U	S	N	O	C	F	B	I
I	U	U	C	E	B	U	N	A	D	N	A
U	S	S	R	E	P	U	B	L	I	C	N
S	R	T	S	U	F	F	E	C	T	S	L
D	O	M	I	T	I	A	N	T	O	G	A

34 Latin to English crossword

	A		I		I		H		T		
B	L	A	C	K	S	M	I	T	H	S
	L		U		T		S		E		
B	E	S	T		A		S	A	Y	S
	M				Y				M		
S	P	E	A	R		W	E	S	A	Y
	E				W				Y		
F	R	O	M		O		I	A	S	K
	O		U		R		L		E		
P	R	O	C	E	S	S	I	O	N	S
	S		H		T		E		D		

35 English to Latin crossword

	U		O			H		D	
E	X	I	M	U	S		O	P	U	S
	O		N		P	C		C	
O	R	D	I	N	E	S		E	O	S
	E		U		R		A		I	
A	M	E	M		A		D	E	N	T
M		D			N		O		O	
A	V	E		E	D	I	M	I	N	I
	I		L		U		I		F	
V	A	L	E		S	E	N	T	I	S
	S		O			O		T	

36 Why?

P	U	L	C	H	R	I	O	R	E	M
E		U		A			E		A	
R	I	D	E	N	T		E	D	O	R
S		O		C	U	R		D		I
U			H		I		S	I	N	T
A		V	I	A		F	I	S		I
D	E	I	S		T		M			E
E		D		Q	U	A		V		B
A	D	E	S		A	U	D	I	A	R
N		A				L		N		I
T	E	M	P	E	R	A	M	I	N	I

71

37 You're falling

```
A L I A   ▓ D A R E
P ▓ ▓ ▓ C ▓ ▓ ▓ X
E ▓ C L A M A ▓ I
R ▓ A ▓ D ▓ N ▓ T
▓ B E N I G N O ▓
N ▓ C ▓ T ▓ O ▓ N
A ▓ A L I U S ▓ A
V ▓ ▓ ▓ S ▓ ▓ ▓ V
E I U S ▓ M U R I
```

38 Sudoku

IV	VI	II	V	IX	III	I	VIII	VII
IX	VII	III	VI	I	VIII	V	IV	II
V	VIII	I	II	IV	VII	III	VI	IX
VII	III	IV	I	VIII	II	IX	V	VI
VIII	V	VI	IV	III	IX	II	VII	I
II	I	IX	VII	VI	V	VIII	III	IV
I	IX	VII	VIII	V	IV	VI	II	III
VI	IV	VIII	III	II	I	VII	IX	V
III	II	V	IX	VII	VI	IV	I	VIII

39 Latin to English crossword

```
B E S T G L A D I A T O R
Y ▓ H ▓ ▓ ▓ M ▓ ▓ ▓ H ▓ U
S H E M A Y P R O C E E D
C ▓ M ▓ ▓ ▓ H ▓ ▓ ▓ Y ▓ E
H ▓ A ▓ S H I P S ▓ S ▓ A
O ▓ Y ▓ L ▓ T ▓ L ▓ A ▓ N
O F T H E S H O U T I N G
L ▓ E ▓ E ▓ E ▓ G ▓ L ▓ R
T ▓ R ▓ P L A N S ▓ A ▓ Y
O ▓ R ▓ ▓ ▓ T ▓ ▓ ▓ L ▓ E
S O I H E A R A S T O R Y
I ▓ F ▓ ▓ ▓ E ▓ ▓ ▓ N ▓ E
T O Y O U R S T R E E T S
```

40 English to Latin crossword

```
▓ O ▓ R ▓ I ▓ D ▓ E ▓ P
A M P H I T H E A T R U M
▓ N ▓ E ▓ E ▓ S ▓ F ▓ L
L E O N I ▓ V ▓ D I S C O
▓ S ▓ I ▓ N V I T E T ▓ H
S P E ▓ V ▓ R ▓ L ▓ I R E
▓ R ▓ M I L I T E S ▓ I
V I R ▓ T ▓ L ▓ M ▓ C O R
▓ N ▓ C A D I M U S ▓ R
S C I A T ▓ S ▓ R A D I X
▓ I ▓ E ▓ E ▓ N ▓ X ▓ B
S P E C T A T O R I B U S
▓ I ▓ I ▓ S ▓ X ▓ S ▓ S
```

41 Hadrian's places

```
  A Q U I N C U M
P O M E R I U M
    D A C I A
A N T I N O O P O L I S
    B U D A P E S T
C L A U D I O P O L I S
  P U T E O L I
      M A I N Z
A T H E N S
```

The answer: Nicopolis

42 Latin Verbs-only crossword

```
▓ C ▓ F ▓ U ▓ I ▓
H A B U E R A N T
▓ P ▓ I ▓ S ▓ T ▓
S T E T ▓ I E R O
▓ U ▓ ▓ I ▓ ▓ A ▓
E S S E ▓ D A B O
▓ S ▓ S ▓ A ▓ A ▓
M I T T E R E N T
▓ M ▓ O ▓ I ▓ T ▓
```

43 They know I'm first

S	I	C		G		M		V	I	A
U		O		L		A		I		V
M	U	L	T	A	E	G	I	S	T	I
		L		D		I		I		
A	M	A	V	I	S	S	E	T	I	S
		T		A		T		A		
P	R	A	E	T	O	R	I	B	U	S
		S		O		O		A		
S	C	I	O	R	P	R	I	M	U	S
I		N		E		U		U		U
T	O	T		S		M		S	T	A

44 Who's at the door?

	L		V								C
S	Y	M	M	A	C	H	U	S			I
	C			R			A				N
	O		R	U	F	U	S		U		N
	R			S			P	O	L	L	A
	I						A	U			
	S			S	E	X	T	U	S		C
				A							A
N	A	E	V	I	A	L	I	N	U	S	
	P				E				T		
G	E	M	E	L	L	U	S		O		
	R						M	A	R	O	

The answer: Laecania

45 Martial's mates

A	M	I	C	I		O	M	N	E	S		S	U	N	T

46 Campaigns and Politics wordsearch

N	S	U	C	S	U	F	S	J	L	O	P
E	U	F	T	A	D	I	U	T	R	I	X
R	I	V	N	R	A	S	L	R	S	R	R
V	L	W	O	M	C	E	A	A	U	K	L
A	E	D	I	I	I	R	B	I	N	U	S
C	N	A	G	Z	A	V	E	A	A	A	U
E	R	M	E	E	N	I	C	N	I	Q	N
B	O	N	L	G	X	A	E	U	R	U	A
U	C	A	Q	E	Z	N	D	S	D	I	I
N	C	T	B	T	L	U	S	U	A	N	T
A	V	I	N	H	M	S	K	S	H	C	I
D	M	O	G	U	N	T	I	A	C	U	M
F	Z	O	E	S	C	U	S	K	P	M	O
R	E	G	I	A	S	U	C	I	C	A	D

47 Latin to English crossword

	W		B		T		P		H	
H	E	H	A	D	W	A	L	K	E	D
	W		T		O		A		H	
F	I	G	H	T		A	N	G	E	R
	L		S	H	I	P	S		L	
I	L	L		E		A		S	P	Y
	C		A	R	E	I	N		S	
T	O	O	W	E		N	O	R	T	H
	U		O		S		I		R	
A	G	O	O	D	O	L	D	B	O	Y
	H		D		N		O		Y	

48 It's here

A	D	E	S	T		B	A	R	B	A
R		X		E		I		E		D
I	M	P	E	R	A	B	A	T	I	S
D		L		R		I		I		I
A	M	I	C	A		S	E	N	E	M
		C					E			
A	M	A	T	A		C	I	B	U	M
G		N		L		A		A		I
R	E	D	I	I	S	S	E	M	U	S
O		U		U		T		U		C
S	I	M	U	S		I	I	S	S	E

49 Sudoku

VIII	II	VI	III	I	IX	IV	V	VII
V	IX	I	VI	IV	VII	II	III	VIII
VII	III	IV	II	V	VIII	I	IX	VI
I	VII	IX	IV	VIII	V	VI	II	III
II	VI	VIII	IX	III	I	VII	IV	V
III	IV	V	VII	VI	II	IX	VIII	I
IX	V	II	VIII	VII	VI	III	I	IV
VI	VIII	III	I	II	IV	V	VII	IX
IV	I	VII	V	IX	III	VIII	VI	II

50 ArrowWord

	M		N		C	U	M		
C	E	D	E	R	E			N	O	N
	L		C		C		T		M	E
L	I	M	A	C	I		R		N	
	O		V		D		A		E	
	R	E	I		E		N	O	S	
	I		S		R		S		E	
	B		T		I	N	F	E	R	T
T	U		I		M		I		U	
E	S	T			U	R	G	E	N	T
			A	R	S		I		T	

51 Latin to English crossword

W	I	T	H	S	C	H	O	O	L	S
E		O		H		A		N		H
S	O		S	E	L	L	S		H	E
E		T		S		L		I		P
E	X	E	C	U	T	I	O	N	E	R
Y		A		S		S		D		E
O	F	R	E	P	U	B	L	I	C	S
U		S		E		U		N		E
N	O		A	C	T	I	T		I	N
O		U		T		L		A		T
W	E	P	A	S	S	T	I	M	E	S

52 English to Latin crossword

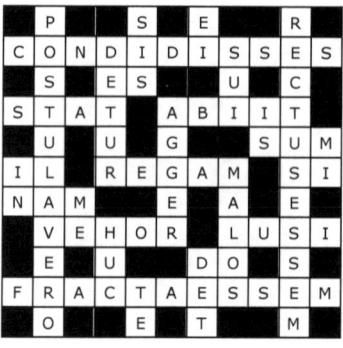

	P		S		E			R	
C	O	N	D	I	D	I	S	S	E	S
	S		E	S			U		C	
S	T	A	T		A	B	I	I	T	
	U		U		G			S	U	M
I	L		R	E	G	A	M		S	I
N	A	M			E		A		E	
	V	E	H	O	R		L	U	S	I
	E		U			D	O		S	
F	R	A	C	T	A	E	S	S	E	M
	O			E		T			M	

53 All done

	O		C	E	R	V	I		A	
S	P	E	R	A		I	N	F	E	R
	E		E			T		G		
A	R	I	D	A		O	R	A	R	E
D	A		O	C	U	L	O		A	B
D			T		E			R	
I	T		F	U	E	R	O		E	I
S	O	L	A	M		E	R	A	S	I
	T		C			B		S	
D	U	C	I	S		T	E	N	E	O
	M		S	I	M	U	S		T	

54 Sudoku

IV	VI	IX	VIII	V	III	II	VII	I
III	I	VII	II	IV	VI	IX	V	VIII
V	VIII	II	I	IX	VII	III	IV	VI
VI	IV	I	V	VII	II	VIII	IX	III
VII	III	V	VI	VIII	IX	IV	I	II
II	IX	VIII	IV	III	I	V	VI	VII
I	II	IV	III	VI	V	VII	VIII	IX
IX	V	III	VII	I	VIII	VI	II	IV
VIII	VII	VI	IX	II	IV	I	III	V

55 Martial wordsearch

```
G C F A C O R D U S U R
M A T Q B S Z E D X U H
A E L R P A U L A F H V
R Y H L J S S L U O L P
O E S D A S A S W L Q H
D S U R A V A F A K L I
S C C R E T T B I B M L
U Z C T R T H A I S G E
M D A S I U S N S N S R
U E L N O R T A S Y U O
T W F R N W V E R E L S
S H T Q U I E V A R U T
O J R G S U C I T T A D
P R I S C U S A R F K E
```

56 They'll love it

```
V U L T █ G E R O
E █ █ B █ █ P
N █ F I A N T █ T
I █ A R █ A █ O
█ A M A B U N T █
P █ A █ A G █ O
A █ E B R I O █ M
R █ █ I █ █ N
S E D E █ H A B E
```

57 Latin to English crossword

```
█ Y █ O █ I █ I █ O █ S █
Y O U W I L L S U F F E R
█ U █ E █ O █ I █ I █ E █
T H I S █ S I T █ T I M E
█ A █ I T █ S O █ S █
O V I D S █ A █ N O R T H
█ E █ I █ A N D █ N █ O
I S I N G █ Y █ T E A C H
█ T █ O F █ D O █ O █
C A M P █ A X E █ F A M E
█ Y █ L █ I █ E █ L █ M
W E W A N T E D T O S I T
█ D █ Y █ H █ S █ W █ T
```

58 English to Latin crossword

```
█ C █ Q █ C █ R █ C █ V █
S A L U T A V E R A M U S
█ L █ O █ E █ V █ N █ L █
P A R S █ L E O █ I G N E
█ M █ █ U █ C █ █ E █
C I R C U M █ A F F E R O
█ T █ U █ █ L █ A █
T A U R U M █ C R E A T E
█ T █ █ O █ U █ U █
T I B I █ V I R █ U R S A
█ B █ S █ E █ A █ R █ E █
A U C T O R I B U S E S T
█ S █ E █ E █ O █ I █ T █
```

59 Latin to English crossword

```
█ W █ D █ I █ P █ F █ S █ I █
H E M A Y B E A B L E T O B E
█ H █ Y █ E █ L █ E █ E █ U █
C A T S █ L E A V E █ P A I N
█ V █ █ C █ C █ T █ █ L █
P E R I S H █ E █ S E N A T E
█ A █ S █ A S H █ O █ A █
A B A N D O N █ I T S E E M S
█ A █ O █ D I D █ N █ O █
S N A T C H █ D █ W E D E N Y
█ D █ U █ O E █ U █
T O M B █ M O N T H █ H O M E
█ N █ E █ A A █ E A █ E █
H E W A S N O T W A N T I N G
█ D █ R █ S E █ R E █ T █
```

60 Double whammy Latin crossword

```
N E M O █ C █ S █ O █ M E U S
O █ A █ C A N T A V I █ Q █ U
T A L E █ S █ R █ E █ I U V A
A █ I S █ A Q U A M █ D O █ E
█ A █ █ █ T █ █ █ F
A N N O █ A D H O C █ M A R E
█ I █ D █ M █ I U █ E █ A
I M P E R A T O R I E R A N T
U █ R █ V █ C █ D █ U █ G
I L L O █ I R A T O █ M E O S
█ A █ █ █ M █ █ █ R
P █ I D █ F R E N A █ E O █ E
A L T A █ A █ L █ D █ S P E S
N █ E █ A T T U L I T █ U █ S
I U R O █ A █ S █ T █ E S T E
```

ALSO AVAILABLE - IMPERIUM LATIN COURSE

The Imperium Latin course has been written for the twenty-first century; unique, highly resourced and written to make fullest use of modern technology. Its texts follow the life of the Emperor Hadrian, from his early childhood to his later years, as he became the most powerful man in the Roman world.

Imperium was released for general use in 2013, after a trialling period of six years. It consists of three coursebooks, a Grammar and Syntax Guide and the Imperium Latin Unseens collection for advanced users. All of these texts can be ordered through Amazon but are also available as pdf files in either one of our two Site Support Packs, which can be bought by schools. The coursebooks are also available as free of charge downloadable pdf files, from the TES Resources website.

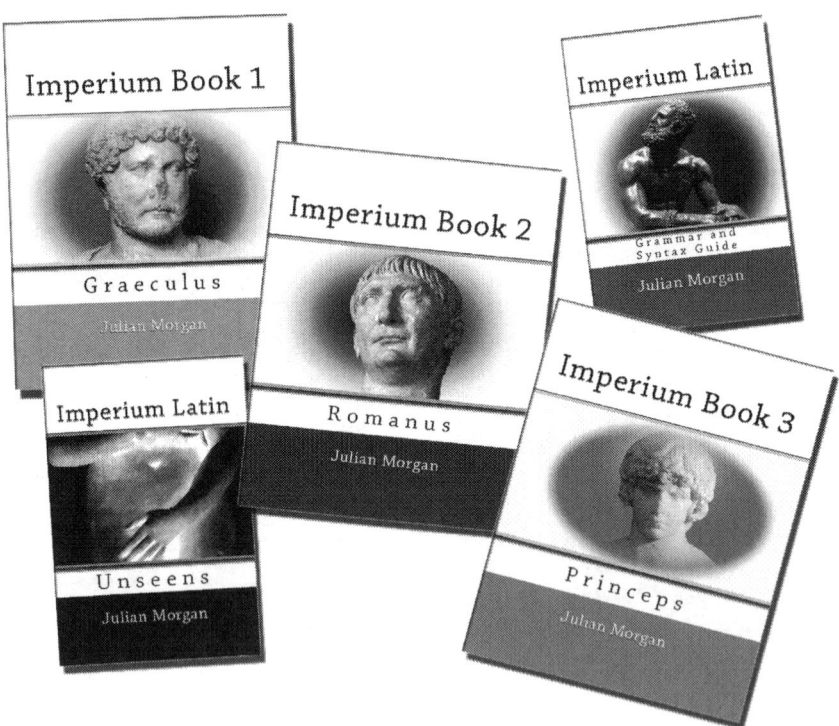

For further details, see www.imperiumlatin.com

PUZZLE BOOKS FROM J-PROGS

These collections of 50 puzzles each are aimed at those who want to have some fun with the languages they once learned, as well as those beginners who want to face the challenges they offer.

Easy Latin Puzzles was written after compiling three lists of words commonly used in a variety of Latin courses. It makes very limited use of word endings and includes a variety of challenges, including sudokus, word searches, Latin to English crosswords and English to Latin ones. The book includes the full word listings used at the back, as well as solutions.

Easy Greek Puzzles has been based around two short lists of words commonly used in a variety of courses. It uses all five cases of noun, adjective and pronoun systems, as well as the active indicative verb endings from the present, imperfect, perfect and future tenses. As such, it will be appropriate for use by those who have studied the language for around one year or longer. Like its companion, it features sudokus, word searches, Greek to English crosswords and English to Greek ones.

For details on how to get your copies, see www.j-progs.com

ABOUT THE AUTHOR

Julian Morgan served as a teacher and a Head of Classics for many years in the UK, before taking up a post in 2007 at the European School of Karlsruhe in Germany. Julian has devoted his entire career to finding new, original ways of teaching Latin and Greek.

Julian has written many educational software titles and books in the last 25 years, publishing many of these under the banner of his business, J-PROGS. He is well known in Classics teaching circles for his teacher training activities, not least in directing courses for the CIRCE Project, which has been part of the EU's Comenius programme since 2003. He has served twice as a Council member of the Joint Association of Classical Teachers and has also been a long-standing member on the Computing Applications Committee of the American Classical League.

He can often be found walking his dogs in the vineyards of Alsace, where he lives.

You can find out more on Julian's Author Page:
amazon.com/author/julianmorgan

Made in the USA
Charleston, SC
10 March 2016